SAMPLE

The Weather Is Here,
Wish You Were Beautiful:
Quotations for the Thoughtful Traveler
by Gordon S. Jackson
ISBN: 978-1-887140-86-7

192 pages   5 ¼ x 7 ¼   Index   Bibliography
$15.95   11 b/w illustrations
Case bound with Dust Jacket
Published: Fall 2009

TO ORDER CONTACT:
NBN Books
1-800-462-6420 • fax: 1-800-338-4550
custserv@nbnbooks.com
or your favorite wholesaler

For additional information, contact: Sally Bahner
SallyB@intrepidtraveler.com
203-469-0214 • fax: 203-469-0430

Published by The Intrepid Traveler, POB 531, Branford, CT 06405

The Weather Is Here, Wish You Were Beautiful

Quotations for the Thoughtful Traveler

Compiled by
Gordon S. Jackson

P.O. Box 531, Branford, CT 06405

The Weather Is Here, Wish You Were Beautiful
Quotations for the Thoughtful Traveler
Published by
The Intrepid Traveler
P. O. Box 531
Branford, CT 06405
http://www.intrepidtraveler.com

Copyright © 2010 by Gordon S. Jackson
First edition
Printed in the U.S.A.
Cover and interior design by Jana Rade
ISBN: 978-1-887140-86-7
Library of Congress Control Number: 2009922205

10 9 8 7 6 5 4 3 2 1

The weather is here, wish you were beautiful : quotations
  for the thoughtful traveler / compiled by Gordon S.
  Jackson.—1st ed.
    p. cm.
    Includes bibliographical references and index.
    LCCN 2009922205
    ISBN-13: 978-1-887140-86-7
    ISBN-10: 1-887140-86-7

    1. Travel—Quotations, maxims, etc.   I. Jackson,
  Gordon, 1949-

  PN6084.T7W43 2009   910
                       QBI09-200035

For Sue, Sarah and Matthew,
the best of traveling companions,
and for Ron Pyle, who knows why

Table of Contents

Acknowledgments

No book is a solo venture and this volume too is indebted to the help of others: those individuals who had a direct impact on its formation, and those whose indirect role was equally indispensible. The first category includes Gail Fielding, at the Whitworth University library, for her crucial role in once again helping me to track down books on inter-library loan. Another Whitworth colleague, Dr. Ginny Whitehouse, and a friend, Stuart McTavish, also were helpful in connecting me with useful resources. Then, my wife, Sue, helped by reading the draft, catching error after error, and asking astute questions that helped me refine the manuscript. My thanks to each of them.

The second, and even more crucial, category of those who have helped shape this book are those countless travelers who over the centuries have recorded their reactions to their experiences, and the compilers of the travel and quotes anthologies listed at the end of the book. Without this vast body of material, and the efforts of so many to record their thoughts throughout the ages, this book would not be possible.

I must also thank the National Geographic Glimpse (formerly The Glimpse Foundation) for permission to reprint several student insights and other useful items from its "Glimpse Study Abroad Acclimation Guides." Thanks too for permission from Paul Fussell to reprint several of his insights from The Norton Book of Travel and other sources. With respect to the remaining quotations, great care has been taken to honor the fair use doctrine in copyright law. If any inadvertent omissions have occurred in this regard, these will be addressed in possible future editions of this book.

Introduction

Travel and exploration are as old as humankind. Whether it is the story of Odysseus, the adventures of Marco Polo, or your family's trip to Europe last summer, throughout history we humans have yearned to travel, explore and discover the new. Well, many of us. And this book is intended for those of us who are both eager to seek out the new, and willing to commit the time, funds and sheer mental energy needed to head to unfamiliar territory, whether in our own country or beyond.

Twenty-first century travel would be utterly unrecognizable to our forebears from even a hundred years back, let alone someone like Odysseus. The trappings of travel have been revolutionized in our time, with our ability to get money from an ATM in Ankara, airport security lines in Seattle, or cruise ships by the dozens in the Caribbean. Yet some things about travel never change: The encounter with another culture where you don't know the language or the customs; the recognition yet again of the humanity we share with people even in settings utterly different from our own; or the profound reality that travel makes us different, deeper, and – if we're fortunate – possibly even a bit wiser.

This volume does not attempt to be a "how to" guide to travel; nor does it pretend to offer the definitive word on the joys and hardships of travel. Rather, its goal is to provide a collection of quotes that will appeal to the thoughtful traveler. The collection, which is intended simply to stretch your thinking about the experience of travel, is divided into five parts: an overview of the reasons we travel, a focus on the journey itself, the difficulties associated with travel, people, and the recognition that travel isn't for everyone. The quotes cover a wide range of travel-related topics, such as the nature of travel, its impact and rewards, language and cultural differences, getting lost, general advice, and some tongue-in-cheek "laws" of travel. The quotes vary in tone from thoughtful to humorous, from literary to practical.

Where do the quotes come from? Besides selections from my own quotes on travel that I have collected over the years, I have scoured both scholarly and popular books on travel, as well as scores of other anthologies of quotations. (See the separate list of sources provided at the end of this book.) This compilation is therefore indebted to the insights and observations of hundreds of other writers and thinkers over the ages. The quotes are almost entirely from print sources, with only a few from some of the more authoritative Internet sites.

Some of the quotes will be familiar; most will not. Included is Robert Frost's well known inspiration to choose "the road less traveled by." But there's also the lesser known but equally vivid picture from Thurston Clark, who asks, "What child has not traveled by spinning a globe?" Or Clifton Fadiman's observation that goes to the heart of travel abroad, and the inevitable dislocation it brings: "To feel at home, stay at home. A foreign country is not designed to make you comfortable. It's designed to make its own people comfortable."

But whether you recognize them or not, all the quotes have been selected for their potential to remind you of important ideas, introduce you to new thoughts and perspectives, or in some other way keep piquing your interest in what others have said about travel. The book therefore lends itself to general reading, pick-up-and-put-down browsing, or even use as a reference tool.

Although this anthology is not intended as a scholarly work, I have put a high premium on accuracy and tried to obtain the most authoritative version of each quote. Likewise, where a quote is attributed to more than one individual, I have relied on the source that appears most authoritative.

I also have tried to include quotes from a wide range of national and cultural perspectives but relatively few quotations come from non-Western speakers or writers. The reason is not that U.S. and British sources are the only ones qualified to speak on this topic. Far from it. It is simply that written quotes from non-Western, and non-English, sources are harder to find.

Then there is the issue of inclusive language. Some quotes use "man," "mankind" and so on when referring to people in general. These quotes reflect earlier usage which characterizes contemporary English less and less. In keeping with the volume's commitment to presenting the quotes as accurately as possible, I have included these entries with their original wording. In a concession to the need for consistency, I have changed the British spelling of "traveller" to "traveler." Most of the sources are given without any further details, but where I thought it would be helpful to understand the context I have added either a description of the source or indicated the date.

Anyone exploring the literature on travel that enriches our libraries and bookstores must come away humbled at its vastness. This book thus does not for a moment pretend to be a definitive anthology of quotes on the subject. Rather, it is a highly personal selection of those items that, for whatever reason, struck me as worthy of inclusion. The category titled

"Destinations: Noteworthy or Not," for instance, was even more subjective than most. It contains no more than a sampling of the thousands upon thousands of repeatable things (good and bad) that people have said about places they have visited.

Two categories ended up with a more negative, even cynical, tone than I expected. Given the state of air travel, especially after 9/11, it is perhaps not surprising that hardly anyone has anything kind to say about this industry or the experience of flying. While the quotes in the section titled "Planes and Trains and..." speak for themselves, let us separate these sentiments from those thousands of individuals working in the industry as pilots, flight attendants, ground crew and others, who get millions of us safely from points A to B each year and, most of the time, our luggage as well.

A second often negative section is that on "Tourists and Tourism." These entries too speak for themselves. The intent of including them, however, was not to pour scorn on the worst aspects of tourism. Instead, it was to commend the tourist for at least taking that first step, of leaving home, but also to prod him or her into asking, "Why settle for clinging to your own culture and the familiar, and even trying to take that with you, when there's so much to experience and learn?"

As Lance Morrow said, "People travel because it teaches them things they could learn no other way." So, regardless of how you use this volume, I hope that with Morrow's observation in mind, this collection of quotes will better prepare you for your own travels, serve as a thoughtful companion on the journey, and help you reflect even more richly on your explorations when you return home.

WHY WE TRAVEL

"Travel is the sherbet between courses of reality."

The Nature of Travel

Away from home you can tell as many lies as you wish.
— **Arab proverb**

The world is a book and those who do not travel read only a page.
— **Augustine**

The whole object of travel is not to set foot on foreign land; it is at last to set foot on one's own country as foreign land.
— **G. K. Chesterton**

Traveling is almost like talking with men of other centuries.
— **René Descartes**

One of the essential skills for a traveler is the ability to make a rather extravagant fool of oneself.
— **John Flinn**

Travel still suggests "travail" to those who know that by leaving home they risk wire-walking without a net.
— **Keath Fraser**

Americans have always been eager for travel, that being how they got to the New World in the first place.
— **Otto Friedrich**

Two roads diverged in a wood, and I —
I took the one less traveled by,
And that has made all the difference.
— **Robert Frost**

The fool wanders, the wise man travels.
— **Thomas Fuller**

But travel is work. Etymologically a traveler is one who suffers travail, a word

deriving in turn for Latin tripalium,
*a torture instrument consisting of three
stakes designed to rack the body.*

— **Paul Fussell**

*To travel is to discover that everyone is
wrong about other countries.*

— **Aldous Huxley**

*A good traveler has no fixed plans, and is
not intent on arriving.*

— **Lao Tzu**

*Travel is sweet because it doesn't wear out
its welcome, bittersweet because it puts time
and place in perspective and reminds us
how small we are.*

— **Nan Levinson**

*A good traveler is one who does not know
where he is going to, and a perfect traveler
does not know where he came from.*

— **Lin Yutang**

*[Travel seems] not just a way of having
a good time, but something that every
self-respecting citizen ought to
undertake, like a high-fiber diet,
say, or a deodorant.*

— **Jan Morris**

*A man of ordinary talent will always be
ordinary, whether he travels or not;
but a man of superior talent . . .
will go to pieces if he remains forever
in the same place.*

— **Wolfgang Amadeus Mozart**

*Travel, at its best, is a process of
continually conquering disbelief.*

— **Michael Palin**

*When a person spends all this time in
foreign travel, he ends by having many
acquaintances but no friends.*

— **Seneca**

How can you be satisfied with yourself if you leave this world without having seen it, although you were in a position to see it?
— **Ahmad Faris al-Shidyaq**

All travel is a quest, conscious or unconscious searching for something that is lacking in our lives or ourselves.
— **Freya Stark**

Traveling is like flirting with life. It's like saying, "I would stay and love you, but I have to go; this is my station."
— **Lisa St. Aubin de Terán**

Travel is ninety percent anticipation and ten percent recollection.
— **Edward Streeter**

In order to travel one must have a home, and one that is loved and pulling a little at the heart-strings all the while; for the best thing about traveling is going home.
— **Charles Dudley Warner**

Exploration, Adventure & Discovery

My favorite thing is to go where I've never been.
— **Diane Arbus**

They are ill discoverers that think there is no land, when they can see nothing but sea.
— **Francis Bacon**

On arrival at a Syrian port the traveler's passport is sometimes asked for, but an ordinary visiting card will answer the purpose equally well.
— **Karl Baedeker**
(in *Guide to Palestine and Syria*, 1876)

All journeys have secret destinations of
which the traveler is unaware.
— **Martin Buber**

Most people think they have too many
responsibilities to travel, especially in the way
that appeals to their fantasies. The hungry spouse,
children, job, mortgage, school, army or mother
needs them. This is bullshit, of course. Most people
are simply too afraid to step out of the rut to do
something they would like to do. Honest, folks.
The world doesn't end when you decide to do
what you want to do, it merely begins.
— **Ed Buryn**

Exploring is delightful to look forward to
and back upon, but it is not comfortable at
the time, unless it be of such an easy nature
as not to deserve the name.
— **Samuel Butler**

Most of us abandoned the idea of
a life full of adventure and travel
sometime between puberty and our

first job. Our dreams die under
the dark weight of responsibility.
Occasionally the old urge surfaces,
and we label it with names that
suggest psychological aberrations: the
big chill, a mid-life crisis.
— **Tim Cahill**

"Would you tell me, please, which way I
ought to go from here?"
"That depends a good deal on where you
want to get to," said the Cat.
— **Lewis Carroll**

If you have the desire for knowledge and
the power to give it physical expression, go
out and explore.
— **Apsley Cherry-Garrard**

An adventure is only an inconvenience
rightly considered. An inconvenience is only
an adventure wrongly considered.
— **G. K. Chesterton**

What child has not traveled by spinning a globe?
— **Thurston Clarke**

*Along this track of pathless ocean it is my
intention to steer.*
— **Christopher Columbus**

Following the sun we left the old world.
— **Christopher Columbus**
(an inscription on one of his caravels)

*Adventures are an indication of inefficiency.
Good explorers don't have them.*
— **Herbert Spencer Dickey**

*Only those who will risk going too far can
possibly find out how far one can go.*
— **T. S. Eliot**

*We shall not cease from our explorations
And the end of all our exploring
Will be to arrive where we started
And know the place for the first time.*
— **T. S. Eliot**

Only the air-spirits know
What lies beyond the hills,
Yet I urge my team farther on
Drive on and on
On and on!
— **Eskimo poem**

Adventure is really a soft option....
It requires far less courage to be
an explorer than to be a chartered
accountant.
— **Peter Fleming**

That is the charm of a map.
It represents the other side of the horizon,
where everything is possible.
— **Rosita Forbes**

We must go beyond textbooks, go
out into the bypaths and untrodden
depths of the wilderness and travel
and explore and tell the world the
glories of our journey.
— **John Hope Franklin**

One does not discover new lands without consenting to lose sight of the shore for a very long time.
— **André Gide**

Can I learn to look at things with clear, fresh eyes? How much can I take in at a single glance? Can the grooves of mental habits be effaced?
— **Johann Wolfgang von Goethe**

I am always ready to visit a new place.
— **Graham Greene**

He that goeth far hath many encounters.
— **George Herbert**

Not bound to swear allegiance to any master, wherever the wind takes me I travel as a visitor.
— **Horace**

Everything in Africa bites, but the safari bug is worst of all.
— **Brian Jackman**

Have you never questioned travelers? Do you not accept the evidence they bring...?

— **Job 21:29**
(Revised English Bible)

Allah has laid out the earth for you like a vast carpet so that you will travel its endless roads.

— **The Koran**

We are now about to penetrate a country at least two thousand miles in width, on which the foot of civilized man has never trodden; the good or evil it has in store for us was for experiment yet to determine.... Entertaining as I do the most confident hope of succeeding in a voyage which had formed a darling project of mine for the last ten years, I could but esteem this moment of my departure as among the most happy of my life.

— **Meriwether Lewis**
(co-leader of the Lewis and Clark expedition, 1804)

Travelers are always discoverers, especially those who travel by air. There are no signposts in the sky to show a man has passed that way before. There are no channels marked. The flier breaks each second into new uncharted seas.
— **Anne Morrow Lindbergh**

The whole world is full of things, and somebody has to look for them.
— **Astrid Lindgren**

I am excessively weak, and but for the donkey, could not move a hundred yards. It is not all pleasure, this exploration.
— **David Livingstone**

The first question which you will ask and which I must try to answer is this, "What is the use of climbing Mount Everest" and my answer must at once be, "It is no use." ... We shall not bring back a single bit of gold or silver, not a gem, nor any coal or iron. We shall not find a single foot of earth that can be planted with crops to raise food. It's no use. So, if you cannot understand that there is something in man which responds to the challenge of this mountain and goes out to meet it, that the struggle is the struggle of life itself upward and forever upward, then you won't see why we go.

— **George Mallory**
(before his fatal attempt on Mount Everest, 1922)

I love to sail forbidden seas, and land on barbarous coasts.

— **Herman Melville**

Everybody in 15th century Spain was wrong about where China was and as a result, Columbus discovered Caribbean vacations.

— **P. J. O'Rourke**

Oh the places you'll go!

— **Dr. Seuss**

Sometimes one must travel far to discover what is near.

— **Uri Shulevitz**

*I could not comprehend in the least
what lay before us … Yet it is our
destiny to move on, whatever direction
it may be that narrow winding path,
running among tall grasses and down
into gullies and across small streams,
takes us, until we penetrate that cold,
dark, still horizon before us.*

— **Henry Morton Stanley**

*I have traveled widely in my lifetime,
having been struck by the virus at an
early age and having, as yet, developed no
antibodies to harden my resistance
or immunity.*

— **Caskie Stinnett**

*As light and the day are free to all men, so
nature has left all lands open to brave men.*

— **Tacitus**

*You can't cross the sea merely by standing
and staring at the water.*

— **Rabindranath Tagore**

I cannot rest from travel.
— **Alfred Lord Tennyson**

For me, exploration was a personal venture. I did not go to the Arabian desert to collect plants nor to make a map; such things were incidental. At heart I knew that to write or even talk of my travels was to tarnish the achievement. I went there to find peace in the hardship of desert travel and the company of desert people. I set myself a goal on these journeys, and, although the goal itself was unimportant, its attainment had to be worth every effort and sacrifice.
— **Wilfred Thesiger**

Not all those who wander are lost.
— **J. R. R. Tolkien**

Remember what Bilbo used to say: It's a dangerous business, Frodo, going out your door. You step onto the road, and if you don't keep your feet, there's no knowing where you might be swept off to.
— **J. R. R. Tolkien**

Twenty years from now you will be more disappointed by the things you didn't do than by the ones you did. So throw off the bowlines. Sail away from the safe harbor. Catch the trade winds in your sails. Explore. Dream. Discover.

— **Mark Twain**

If we do not find anything pleasant, at least we shall find something new.

— **Voltaire**

When you're safe at home you wish you were having an adventure; when you're having an adventure, you wish you were safe at home.

— **Thornton Wilder**

Make voyages! Attempt them. There's nothing else.

— **Tennessee Williams**

I have discovered that most of the beauties of travel are due to the strange hours we keep to see them.

— **William Carlos Williams**

Travels Impact & Rewards

The traveled mind is the catholic mind,
educated out of exclusiveness and egotism.
— **A. B. Alcott**

Human beings everywhere are more
alike than unalike, and what is
true anywhere is true everywhere,
yet I encourage travel to as many
destinations as possible for the sake
of education as well as pleasure.
— **Maya Angelou**

Perhaps travel cannot prevent bigotry,
but by demonstrating that all peoples cry,
laugh, eat, worry, and die, it can introduce

the idea that if we try and understand each other, we may even become friends.
— **Maya Angelou**

He who has not traveled does not know the value of a man.
— **Arab proverb**

Who lives sees much.
Who travels sees more.
— **Arab proverb**

I met a lot of people in Europe.
I even encountered myself.
— **James Baldwin**

We wander for distraction but we travel for fulfillment.
— **Hilaire Belloc**

But we have tasted wild fruit, listened to strange music; And all shores of the earth are but as doors of an inn.
— **Lawrence Binyon**

Travel has been the universal catalyst. It has made men think faster, imagine larger, want more passionately. The returning traveler brings home disturbing ideas. Pascal (three centuries before television) said that men's ills came from the fact that he had not yet learned to sit quietly in a room.

— **Daniel Boorstin**

What gives value to travel is fear. It is a fact that, at a certain moment, when we are so far from our own country … we are seized by a vague fear, and an instinctive desire to go back to the protection of old habits. This is the most obvious benefit of travel … There is no pleasure in traveling, and I look upon it more as an occasion for spiritual testing.

— **Albert Camus**

They say travel broadens the mind; but you must have the mind.

— **G. K. Chesterton**

How much a dunce that has been sent to roam
Excels a dunce that has been kept at home.
— **William Cowper**

I think wherever you go becomes
a part of you somehow.
— **Anita Desai**

Travel teaches toleration.
— **Benjamin Disraeli**

Too often travel, instead of broadening the
mind, merely lengthens the conversation.
— **Elizabeth Drew**

The freedom to travel safely and cheaply
is one of the great blessings of our time
— something that immeasurably expands
the range of human experience.
— **Michael Elliott**

The crow went traveling abroad and came
back just as black.
— **English proverb**

Traveling makes one modest. You see what a tiny place you occupy in the world.
— **Gustave Flaubert**

Travel is one way of lengthening life.
— **Benjamin Franklin**

Travel makes a wise man better but a fool worse.
— **Thomas Fuller**

The anthropologist Claude Lévi-Strauss notes that a traveler takes a journey not just in space and time (most travel being to places more ancient than the traveler's home) but "in the social hierarchy as well"; and he has noticed repeatedly that upon arriving in a new place he has suddenly become rich (travelers to Mexico, China or India will know the feeling).
— **Paul Fussell**

Travel sharpens the senses. Abroad, one feels, sees and hears things in an abnormal way.
— **Paul Fussell**

[T]ravel is a vivid experience for most of us. At home we have lost the capacity to see what is before us. Travel shakes us out of our apathy, and we regain an attentiveness that heightens every experience.
— **John Gardner**

He who never leaves his country is full of prejudices.
— **Carlo Goldoni**
(in 1757)

No man can be a politician, except he be first an historian or a traveler.
— **James Harrington**
(in 1656)

To travel is to possess the world.
— **Burton Holmes**

Some minds improve by travel; others, rather, resemble copper wire or brass, which gets narrower by going farther.
— **Thomas Hood**

Travel suddenly opens the windows of the soul to the reality of God in other people.
— **Eric James**

The use of traveling is to regulate imagination by reality, and, instead of thinking how things may be, to see them as they are.
— **Samuel Johnson**

How ya' gonna keep 'em down on the farm (after they've seen Paree)?
— **Sam M. Lewis and Joe Young**
(song title, 1918)

Not only does travel give us a new system of reckoning, it also brings to the fore unknown aspects of our own self. Our consciousness being broadened and enriched, we shall judge ourselves more correctly.
— **Ella Maillart**

It is but to be able to say that they have been to such a place, or have seen such a thing, that, more than any real taste for it, induces the majority of the world to incur the trouble and fatigue of traveling.

— **Frederick Marryat**

But there is one priceless thing that I brought back from my trip around the world, one that cost no money on which I paid no customs duty: humility, a humility born from watching other people, other races, struggling bravely and hoping humbly for the simplest things in life.

— **Felix Martí-Ibáñez**

As the traveler who has once been from home is wiser ... so a knowledge of one other culture should sharpen our ability to scrutinize more steadily, to appreciate more lovingly, our own.

— **Margaret Mead**

I came back to where I have never been.

— **W. S. Merwin**

If we are always arriving and departing, it is also true that we are eternally anchored. One's destination is never a place but rather a new way of looking at things.

— **Henry Miller**

We travel to learn; and I have never been in any country where they did not do something better than we do it, think some thoughts better than we think, catch some inspiration from heights above our own.

— **Maria Mitchell**

A man travels the world over in search of what he needs and returns home to find it.

— **George Moore**

And this is what the traveler discovers: In this great and endlessly fascinating world of ours, everywhere can be home.

— **Meredith Moraine**

People travel because it teaches them things
they could learn no other way.
— **Lance Morrow**

Traveling is not just seeing the new; it is also
leaving behind. Not just opening doors; also
closing them behind you, never to return. But
the place you have left forever is always there
for you to see whenever you shut your eyes.
— **Jan Myrdal**

I have crossed an ocean
I have lost my tongue
From the root of the old one
A new one has sprung.
— **Grace Nichols**

The books one reads in childhood ... create in one's
mind a sort of false map of the world, a series of
fabulous countries into which one can retreat at
odd moments throughout the rest of life, and which
in some cases can even survive a visit to the real
countries which they are supposed to represent.
— **George Orwell**

Only with travel can a man ripen.
— **Persian proverb**

Change of soil and climate has in it much that is pleasurable.
— **Pliny the Younger**

Travel compels you to discover your spiritual side by simple elimination: Without all the rituals, routines, and possessions that give your life meaning at home, you're forced to look for meaning within yourself.
— **Rolf Potts**

The real voyage of discovery consists not in seeking new landscapes but in having new eyes.
— **Marcel Proust**

Against my will, in the course of my travels, the belief that everything worth knowing was known at Cambridge gradually wore off. In this respect my travels were very useful to me.
— **Bertrand Russell**

To travel is to return to strangers.
— **Dennis Scott**

Voyage, travel and change of place impart vigor.
— **Seneca**

Traveling leads you to encounter the other, which will always be a way of encountering yourself.
— **Luis Sepúlveda**

Traveling teaches us to commit, to take on the problems of others as if they were our own, because they are our own.
— **Luis Sepúlveda**

A man is the happier for life from having made once an agreeable tour.
— **Sydney Smith**

The real measure of travel, like that of a conversation by the fireside, is the discovery of oneself through contact with other people, and its condition is self-commitment in the dialogue.
— **Paul Tournier**

Travel is fatal to prejudice, bigotry and narrow-mindedness, and many of our people need it sorely on these accounts. Broad, wholesome, charitable views of men and things cannot be acquired by vegetating in one little corner of the earth all one's lifetime.

— **Mark Twain**

One of the great things about travel is you find out how many good, kind people there are.

— **Edith Wharton**

THE JOURNEY

*"The flight time today is five hours in first class
and twelve and a half in coach."*

Getting Ready, Setting Off

The great joy in setting out lies entirely in the unexpected.
— **Mariano Azuela**

Make no little plans; they have no magic to stir men's blood.
— **Daniel H. Burnham**

To know the road ahead, ask those coming back.
— **Chinese proverb**

Come to think of it, you can't get there from here.
— **Marshall Dodge and Robert Bryan**

Men who travel should leave their prejudices at home.
— **Frederick Douglass**

Plans are nothing. Planning is everything.
— **Dwight D. Eisenhower**

A bad beginning makes a bad ending.
— **Euripides**

Up, lad: when the journey's over There'll be time enough to sleep.
— **A. E. Houseman**

A journey of a thousand miles must begin with a single step.
— **Lao Tzu**

Is there anything as horrible as starting on a trip? Once you're off, that's all right, but the last moments are earthquake and convulsion, and the feeling that you are a snail being pulled off your rock.
— **Anne Morrow Lindbergh**

One should always have one's boots on and be ready to leave.
— **Michel de Montaigne**

Every journey, great and small, begins with unrealistic expectations.
— **R. J. Montore**

Our plans miscarry because they have no aim. When a man does not know what harbor he is making for, no wind is the right wind.
— **Seneca**

[W]hen one travels, the first step is the beginning of the arrival.
— **Seng Chao**

Crowns in my purse I have and goods at home, And so am come abroad to see the world.
— **William Shakespeare**

A man should know something about his own country, too, before he goes abroad.
— **Laurence Sterne**

"*We want to do the whole Jack Kerouac–'On The Road'
thing, only with B & B.s.*"

On The Road

The journey not the arrival matters.
— **T. S. Eliot**

*How long the road is. But, for all the time the journey
has already taken, how you have needed every second
of it in order to learn what the road passes by.*
— **Dag Hammarskjöld**

*It is such a bewildered, scared feeling to go
for the first time to a place and not know
where to call out to the driver to stop.*
— **Katharine Butler Hathaway**

*A true journey, no matter how long the
travel takes, has no end.*
— **William Least Heat-Moon**

Climate is what you expect.
Weather is what you get.
— **Robert A. Heinlein**
(attributed)

Our battered suitcases were piled on the
sidewalk again; we had longer ways to go.
But no matter, the road is life.
— **Jack Kerouac**

What is the feeling when you're driving away from
people, and they recede on the plain till you see
their specks dispersing? — it's the too huge world
vaulting us, and it's good-bye. But we lean forward
to the next crazy venture beneath the skies.
— **Jack Kerouac**

It is good to have an end to journey toward;
but it is the journey that matters, in the end.
— **Ursula K. Le Guin**

Traveler, there is no path,
paths are made by walking.
— **Antonio Machado**

*The more you ask how much
longer it will take, the longer
the journey seems.*

— **Maori proverb**

*A journey, one hopes, will become
its own justification, will assume
patterns, reveal its possibilities
— reveal, even, its layers of meaning
— as one goes along, trusting to
chance, to instinct, to hunch. When
you start off you do not necessarily
know where you are going or why.*

— **Shiva Naipaul**

*Journal writing and travel go
together like chai and samosas.
Each can stand alone but both are
enhanced by the other.*

— **Mary Orr**

*The simple willingness to improvise is more
vital, in the long run, than research.*

— **Rolf Potts**

The [travel] writer is abroad — away from home, in that state of enhanced alertness that comes from being uprooted from one's natural habitat.
— **Jonathan Raban**

Does the road wind up-hill all the way?
Yes, to the very end.
Will the day's journey take the whole long day?
From morn to night, my friend.
— **Christina Rossetti**

The wise traveler is he who is perpetually surprised.
— **Vita Sackville-West**

He who would travel happily must travel light.
— **Antoine de Saint-Exupéry**

Own only what you can carry with you; know language, know countries, know people. Let your memory be your travel bag.
— **Alexander Solzhenitsyn**

A journey is like marriage. The certain way to be wrong is to think you control it.
— **John Steinbeck**

Once a journey is designed, equipped, and put in process a new factor enters and takes over ... it has personality, temperament, individuality, uniqueness. A journey is a person in itself, no two are alike.
— **John Steinbeck**

To travel hopefully is a better thing than to arrive.
— **Robert Louis Stevenson**

[I]t is not the goal but the way there that matters, and the harder the way the more worthwhile the journey.
— **Wilfred Thesiger**

I had grown into my clothes, the way travelers do who haven't looked in a mirror for weeks.
— **Colin Thubron**

Every journey is a little piece of hell.
— **Tunisian proverb**

All saints can do miracles, but few of them can keep a hotel.
— **Mark Twain**

It used to be a good hotel, but that proves nothing — I used to be a good boy.
— **Mark Twain**

The Laws of Travel

[M]y aunt ... told me I should travel slowly or I would see too much before I died.
— **Sandra Alcosser**

The bigger the terminal, the worse the public address system.
— **Paul Dickson**

When the plane you are on is late, the plane you want to transfer to is on time.
— **Paul Dickson**

Eisenstein's Laws of Tourism. 1. If you go during the season with the best weather, it will be the worst weather in forty-nine years. 2. No matter where you sit, the view out the other side will be better. 3. If you move from a room into another one because something is wrong, something will be worse in the new room. 4. The best trips are the unplanned ones; this way, you won't worry about fouling up your timetable. Conversely, the tighter the timetable, the more you'll worry and the later you'll be.

— **Edward L. Eisenstein**

A good road and a wise traveler are two different things.

— **English proverb**

The heaviest baggage for a traveler is an empty purse.

— **English proverb**
(also attributed to other nationalities)

If you actually look like your passport photo, you aren't well enough to travel.

— **Sir Vivian Fuchs**

*The strength of the turbulence
is directly proportional to the
temperature of your coffee.*

— **Gunter's Second Law of air travel**

*For kings and governments may err
But never Mr. Baedeker*

— **A. P. Herbert**
(commenting on Karl Baedeker,
legendary guidebook author)

*He who has seen one cathedral ten times
has seen something; he who has seen ten
cathedrals once has seen but little; and
he who has spent half an hour in each of
a hundred cathedrals has seen nothing at
all. Four hundred pictures on a wall are
four hundred times less interesting than
one picture, and no one knows a café till
he has gone there often enough to know
the names of the waiters. These are the
laws of travel.*

— **Sinclair Lewis**

*A vacation is having nothing to do
and all day to do it in.*
— **Robert Orben**

*Whatever airline you fly and whichever
airport you fly to, you always land at
Gate 102.*
— **Harold Reis**

Why doesn't it ever rain on museum days?
— **David Shaw**
(from the film "If It's Tuesday, It Must Be Belgium")

*Smock's Travel Observations: 1. Every country
is a "land of contrast." 2. Wherever you travel,
the weather is "unusual for this time of year."*
— **Ruth Smock**

*The distance between the ticket counter
and your plane is directly proportional
to the weight of what you are carrying
and inversely proportional to the time
remaining before takeoff.*
— **Gary Witzenburg**

"Planes and Trains and . . ."

*It can hardly be a coincidence
that no language on earth has ever
produced the expression, "As pretty
as an airport."*
— **Douglas Adams**

*When it comes to flying, I am a nervous
passenger but a confident drinker
and Valium-swallower.*
— **Martin Amis**

*The great difference between voyages rests
not with the ships, but with the people
you meet on them.*
— **Amelia E. Barr**

Travel by sea nearly approximates the bliss of babyhood. They feed you, rock you gently to sleep and when you wake up, they take care of you and feed you again.

— **Geoffrey Bocca**

Airline travel is hours of boredom, interrupted by moments of stark terror.

— **Al Boliska**

Why after all these years do the flight attendants still put a life vest over their heads and show you how to pull the little cord that inflates it? In the entire history of commercial aviation no life has been saved by the provision of a life vest. I am especially fascinated by the way they include a little plastic whistle on each vest. I always imagine myself plunging vertically toward the ocean at 1,200 miles an hour and thinking, "Well, thank gosh I've got this whistle."

— **Bill Bryson**

People in bus terminals look tired even before they start the trip.
— **Jimmy Cannon**

Men travel faster now, but I do not know if they go to better things.
— **Willa Cather**

Whether they take the form of modern metropolitan airports or dusty rural bus stops, terminals are where travelers of all kinds sort themselves out and make ready for the beginnings and endings of their personal journeys. They are places where no one really belongs, intersecting between being home and being someplace else, and as such they are monuments to the human divide between traveling and staying put.
— **Erve Chambers**

The only way of catching a train I ever discovered is to miss the train before.
— **G. K. Chesterton**
(attributed)

I must place on record my regret that the human race ever learned to fly.
— **Winston Churchill**

I'm often unlucky enough to be picked out for those "special searches" due to my obvious resemblance to Mr. bin Laden.
— **Joan Collins**

The limitless jet-lag purgatory of Immigration and Baggage at Heathrow.
— **Monica Dickens**

The time will come when people will travel in stages moved by steam engines, from one city to another, almost as fast as birds can fly, fifteen or twenty miles an hour.
— **Oliver Evans**
(in 1813)

Railway termini: They are our gates to the glorious and the unknown. Through them we pass out into adventure and sunshine, to them, alas! we return.
— **E. M. Forster**

When Byron left England in 1816, he did so in a custom-built coach costing 500 pounds — in a day when a hundred pounds was a decent income. His coach sported a bed, a plate- and cutlery-chest, and a library. But even private and elegant as it was designed to be, by modern standards coach travel ... was physically and socially miserable.

— **Paul Fussell**

Airplane travel is nature's way of making you look like your passport photo.

— **Al Gore**

[H]e won't fly on any airline where the pilots believe in reincarnation.

— **Spalding Gray**

As far as I'm concerned, there are only two kinds of airline bags: carry-on and lost. And in recent years, it's safe to say that things have not gone from bad to worse — they've gone from worse to: Why are you checking your bags on domestic flights?

— **Peter Greenberg**

Food is the most important, most popular thing on a cruise.
— **Gerd Hertel**
(Norwegian Cruise Line executive)

If you are sitting in an exit row and you cannot read this card or cannot see well enough to follow these instructions, please tell a crew member.
— **Instructions on an airplane safety sheet**
(cited by Ken Davis)

Travelers on horseback know nothing of the toil of those who travel on foot.
— **Japanese proverb**

[T]he aeroplane is not capable of unlimited magnification. It is not likely that it will ever carry more than five or seven passengers. High-speed monoplanes will carry even less.
— **Waldemar Kaempfert**
(in a 1913 article on the future of aviation)

If Wilbur and Orville were alive today, Wilbur would have to fire Orville to reduce costs.

— **Herb Kelleher**
(founder of Southwest Airlines)

I feel about airplanes the way I feel about diets. It seems to me that they are wonderful things for other people to go on.

— **Jean Kerr**

The Queen Elizabeth II provides vast amounts of entertainment for an age that has forgotten how to amuse itself unaided.

— **Hans Koning**

Thanks to the interstate highway system, it is now possible to travel across the country from coast to coast without seeing anything.

— **Charles Kuralt**

When you book your flight, follow these simple safety precautions:

· *Avoid airlines whose idea of "in-flight-entertainment" is drumming*
· *Never be taken in by seemingly impressive slogans like "Uzbekistan's Favorite Airline"*
· *Competent pilots do not usually wear nose jewelry at the controls or rub a lucky rabbit's foot just before take-off*

— **Mark Leigh and Mike Lepine**

The accelerating speed at which the landscape passed called for new modes of perception. Early handbooks on railway travel pointed out that you could avoid dizziness or sudden indispositions by avoiding traveling backwards and by not looking out of the window.

— **Orvar Löfgren**

In the space age, man will be able to go around the world in two hours — one hour for flying and the other to get to the airport.

— **Neil McElroy, 1958**
in 1958

*A sure cure for seasickness is
to sit under a tree.*
— **Spike Milligan**

*Restore human legs as a means of travel.
Pedestrians rely on food for fuel and need
no special parking facilities.*
— **Lewis Mumford**

*I would have to say after a lifetime of having
my knees wrapped around my neck and
turbaned men drooling sound asleep on my
shoulder that the most dangerous form of travel
in the third world is the fabled minibus.*
— **Robert Young Pelton**

*The devil himself had probably redesigned
hell in the light of information he had
gained from observing airport layouts.*
— **Anthony Price**

Sure, the next train has gone ten minutes ago.
— *Punch* **magazine**
(cartoon caption, 1871)

If the social history of the world is ever written, the era in which we live will be called the nomadic period. With the advent of ocean steam navigation and the railway system began a traveling mania which has gradually increased until half of the earth's inhabitants, or at least half of its civilized portions, are on the move.

— *Putnam* **magazine, 1868**

It's getting so you can travel cheaper than you can stay at home.

— **Will Rogers**

All travel becomes dull in exact proportion to its rapidity.

— **John Ruskin**

Going by railroad I do not consider as traveling at all; it is merely being "sent" to a place, and very little different from becoming a parcel.

— **John Ruskin**

The rings of Saturn are composed entirely of lost airline luggage.

— **Mark Russell**

If you've got time to spare, go by air.

— **Neville Shute**
(also attributed to others)

Most people sulk in stage-coaches; I always talk.

— **Sydney Smith**

Passenger:
You're one of the stupidest people I've met.
Swissair employee:
And you're one of the nicest gentlemen I've ever come across. But perhaps we're both wrong.

— **Swissair's ideal response to a neurotic passenger**

It is almost axiomatic that the worst trains take you through magical places.

— **Paul Theroux**

You define a good flight by negatives:
you didn't get hijacked, you didn't crash,
you didn't throw up, you weren't late, you
weren't nauseated by the food.
So you're grateful.
— **Paul Theroux**

Everyone loves trains. No one loves British Rail.
— **Sue Thomas**

Our seaport towns have been
turned inside out. Down comes the
Excursion Train with its thousands
… all rushing with one impulse to
the water's edge.
— *The Times* **of London**
(in 1860, the year after the railway reached Torquay)

[T]hat any general system of conveying
passengers [by train] would … go at a
velocity exceeding ten miles an hour, or
thereabouts, is extremely improbable.
— **Thomas Tredgold**
(in 1835)

Americans drive across country as if someone's chasing them.
— **Calvin Trillin**

There is no unhappiness like the misery of sighting land again after a cheerful, careless voyage.
— **Mark Twain**

I'm fed up with it. I'm sick and tired of the delays, tired of the waiting. I'm hanging it up. You can have it. This is my last flight.
— **Unidentified Eastern Airlines pilot**
(quoted by Raymond Davidson)

You're just fifteen gourmet meals from Europe on the world's fastest ship.
— **United States Lines advertisement**

[P]lay cupid to a British baronet and an American actress; ... reason with a passenger who demanded a refund because he lost a day when the ship crossed the

international date line; and hold the hand of a lonely old lady as she lay dying in a hotel in Rome.

— **Unknown cruise director**
(on a round-the-world voyage,
commenting on his experience)

Scenery unlimited! Only the Vista-Dome California Zephyr gives you so much to see, so much to do! You look up, look down, look all around as you enjoy day-long views of the colorful Colorado Rockies and California's famous Feather River Canyon through the High Sierra.

— **U.S. train advertisement, 1950s**

The airplane stays up because it doesn't have the time to fall.

— **Orville Wright**

Encountering Unfamiliar Territory

I flatter myself [that] I have already improved considerably by my travels. First, I can swallow gruel soup, egg soup, and all manner of soups, without making faces much. Secondly, I can pretty well live without tea....

— **Anna Letitia Barbauld**
(in 1785)

[T]he innate physiological makeup of the human animal is such that discomfort of varying degrees occurs in the presence of alien stimuli. Without the normal props of one's own culture, there is unpredictability, helplessness, a threat to self-esteem, and a

general feeling of "walking on ice" — all of which are stress producing.

— **LaRay M. Barna**

We do not need to understand other people and their customs fully to interact with them and learn in the process; it is making the effort to interact without knowing all the rules, improvising certain situations, that allows us to grow.

— **Mary Catherine Bateson**

The entire trip outside of Western culture will be difficult unless you are willing to set aside your assumptions about how life is. Things that you stand on as being ultimate truths may not be ultimate truths in a place you visit, according to the lives of people there. And, for me, that's one of the most valuable things about traveling. When my assumptions are undermined, it helps me know myself and learn what I unconsciously think about life.

— **Linda Besant**

The locusts fried are fairly good to eat.
— **Lady Anne Blunt**
(on her travels in the Arabian desert, 1878)

I am, I flatter myself, completely a citizen of the world. In my travels through Holland, Germany, Switzerland, Italy, Corsica, France, I never felt myself from home.
— **James Boswell**

What affects men sharply about a foreign nation is not so much finding or not finding familiar things; it is rather not finding them in the familiar place.
— **G. K. Chesterton**

Those who visit foreign nations, but associate only with their own countrymen, change their climate but not their customs. They ... return home with traveled bodies, but untraveled minds.
— **Caleb C. Colton**

A traveler's most interesting meals tend to happen by surprise.
— **David Dale**

To feel at home, stay at home. A foreign country is not designed to make you comfortable. It's designed to make its own people comfortable.
— **Clifton Fadiman**

Toto, I've a feeling we're not in Kansas anymore.
— **Dorothy Gale**
(in *The Wizard of Oz*, screenplay by Noel Langley, Florence Ryerson, and Edgar Woolf)

Loud, obese, wealthy, arrogant, ignorant, rude, materialistic, friendly, war-mongering, ethnocentric, environmentally disrespectful and sexually promiscuous.
— **Glimpse Study Abroad Acclimation Guide**
(citing the main stereotypes of Americans that U.S. students encountered while studying abroad)

The best way to find out about the etiquette, social norms, unspoken rules and idiosyncrasies of your host culture is by talking to people who have already lived there. If you know or can locate international students on your campus who are from your host country, talk to them about the challenges they encountered in coming to the United States. This "reverse perspective" can lend you valuable insight into the cultural differences between the United States and your host country.

— **Glimpse Study Abroad Acclimation Guide**

A prudent traveler never disparages his own country.

— **Carlo Goldoni**

Travel is the act of leaving familiarity behind. Destination is merely a by-product of the journey.

— **Eric Hanson**

It is assumed that knowing the location and price of a good hotel and having a road map is about all that is needed to get you from here to wherever you want to go. But it is easier to go to the moon than it is to enter the world of another civilization. Culture — not space — is the greatest distance between two peoples.
— **Jamake Highwater**

Be sensitively aware of the feelings of other people, preventing what might be offensive behavior on your part. This applies very much to photography.
— **International Center for Responsible Tourism**
(from A Code of Ethics for Tourists)

To know how a society functions, transact business at the post office. To know how a society falls apart, fall in love.
— **Nan Levinson**

[T]here are ancient and flourishing civilized societies which have somehow

managed to exist for many centuries and are still in being though they have had no help from the traveler in solving their problems.

— **Walter Lippmann**

I was once asked if I would like to meet the president of a certain country. I said, "No. But I'd love to meet some sheepherders." The sheepherders and taxi drivers are often the most fascinating people.

— **James Michener**

If you reject the food, ignore the customs, fear the religion and avoid the people, you might better stay home. You are like a pebble thrown into water; you become wet on the surface but you are never part of the water.

— **James Michener**

I think that to get under the surface and really appreciate the beauty of any country, one has to go there poor.

— **Grace Moore**

Your new environment makes demands for which you have no ready-made responses; and your responses, in turn, do not seem to produce the desired results.
— **R. W. Nolan**

Culture shock is precipitated by the anxiety that results from losing all our familiar signs and symbols of social intercourse. These signs or cues include the thousand and one ways in which we orient ourselves to the situation of daily life: how to give orders, how to make purchases, when and where not to respond…. All of us depend for our peace of mind and efficiency on hundreds of these cues, most of which we are not consciously aware.
— **Kalervo Oberg**

A good holiday is one spent among people whose notions of time are vaguer than yours.
— **J. B. Priestley**

Half the world does not know how the other half lives.

— **François Rabelais**

I dislike feeling at home when I am abroad.

— **George Bernard Shaw**

[One prevalent assumption was] that all Americans are rich. People asked me to buy cars for them.

— **Dana Shepherd**
(who studied in Cameroon)

Listen and watch. Humility and learning the language beyond "please" and "thank you" means a lot more open doors. Remember that you're the guest in this country and it isn't your place to make the rules, like it or not. Remember you are a guest and be a good one.

— **Renee Storteboom**
(volunteer in Ethiopia)

Wherever you go, you will receive impressions of the places you see and the people you meet. Do not forget that those people will receive impressions of you.

— **Broughton Waddy**

[L]et go of judgmental statements and thoughts. As experienced travelers say, "It's not good or bad, just different." No one drives on the wrong side of the road; in some countries drivers use the left side, in others the right.

— **Thalia Zepatos**

Destinations: Noteworthy, or Not

Time was you could go on an outing to a town barely thirty miles distant from your own and it was like visiting another country.

— **Beryl Bainbridge**

When we think of Switzerland, the picturesque image that springs into our minds is that of men standing on top of Alps wearing comical shorts and make sounds that can only result from a major hormonal imbalance.

— **Dave Barry**

You should definitely visit the Louvre, a world-famous art museum where you can view, at close range, the backs of thousands of other tourists trying to see the Mona Lisa, which actually was stolen in 1978, but the crowd is so dense that it doesn't matter.

— **Dave Barry**

Streets full of water. Please advise.

— **Robert Benchley**
(in a telegram sent from Venice to his editor at *The New Yorker*, Harold Ross)

Rome was a poem pressed into service as a city.

— **Anatole Broyard**

Miami Beach is where neon goes to die.

— **Lenny Bruce**

Traveling is the ruin of all happiness! There's no looking at a building here [in England] after seeing Italy.

— **Fanny Burney**

*The average cooking in the average hotel
for the average Englishman explains to
a large extent the English bleakness and
taciturnity. Nobody can beam and
warble while chewing pressed beef smeared
with diabolical mustard. Nobody can exult
aloud while ungluing from his teeth a
quivering tapioca pudding.*
— **Karel Čapek**

*Venice is like eating an entire box of
chocolate liqueurs at one go.*
— **Truman Capote**

*What's good, thrilling, exciting about
Colorado was produced by God — not the
Denver Chamber of Commerce.*
— **Eugene Cervi**

*I still go to Chartres Cathedral each
year and to the Parthenon every
three years. Very good. Keeps your
standards high.*
— **Lord Kenneth Clark**

*Canada could have enjoyed:
English government, French
culture, and American know-how.
Instead, it ended up with: English
know-how, French government,
and American culture.*

— **John Robert Colombo**

*Since both its national products, snow
and chocolate, melt, the cuckoo clock was
invented solely in order to give tourists
something solid to remember it by.*

— **Alan Coren**
(speaking of Switzerland)

*Overlooking Granada, the Alhambra
presents a hard and unyielding face to the
world, its square towers displaying martial
symmetry. This severity is softened when
you approach from the back, as terraces of
ornate gardens, interspersed with pools of
running water, seek to emulate the shady,
cool gardens of the Koranic heaven.*

— **Steve Davey**

Appreciation, gratitude, affection — these are the qualities Parisians bestow on their parks. Beauty, serenity, tranquility, majesty — these are the rewards they reap in return.
— **Landt Dennis**

Certain places seem to exist mainly because someone has written about them.
— **Joan Didion**

Heaven is an English policeman, a French cook, a German engineer, an Italian lover and everything organized by the Swiss. Hell is an English cook, a French engineer, a German policeman, a Swiss lover and everything organized by an Italian.
— **John Elliott**

There are three wants which can never be satisfied: that of the rich, who wants something more; that of the sick, who wants something different; and that of the traveler, who says "Anywhere but here."
— **Ralph Waldo Emerson**

Don't go back! It isn't there anymore.
Exception: Switzerland.

— **Betty Feazel**

I once spent a year in Philadelphia;
I think it was on a Sunday.

— **W. C. Fields**

I find it hard to say, because when I was
there it seemed to be shut.

— **Clement Freud**
(on being asked if he liked New Zealand)

In Italy for thirty years under the
Borgias they had warfare, terror,
murder, bloodshed — they produced
Michelangelo, Leonardo da Vinci and
the Renaissance. In Switzerland they
had brotherly love, five hundred years of
democracy and peace, and what did they
produce…? The cuckoo clock.

— **Graham Greene**
(a line from the film *The Third Man*, 1949, spoken by
Orson Welles)

All of Stratford, in fact, suggests powdered history — add hot water and stir and you have a delicious, nourishing Shakespeare.

— **Margaret Halsey**

If you are lucky enough to have lived in Paris as a young man, then wherever you go for the rest of your life, it stays with you, for Paris is a movable feast.

— **Ernest Hemingway**

The park achieved a kind of reality. Like these virtual reality games the children are playing with. I told them we were doing this 40 years ago! Disneyland is virtual reality.

— **John Hench**

Concerning Egypt itself I shall extend my remarks to a great length, because there is no country that possesses so many wonders, nor any that has such a number of works that defy description.

— **Herodotus**

He saw the cities of many men and knew their manners.

— **Homer**
(referring to Odysseus)

The sky broke like an egg into full sunset and the water caught fire.

— **Pamela Hansford Johnson**
(on Bruges, Belgium)

A man who has not been in Italy is always conscious of an inferiority, from his not having seen what it is expected a man should see.

— **Samuel Johnson**

When a man is tired of London, he is tired of life; for there is in London all that life can afford.

— **Samuel Johnson**

Worth seeing? Yes, but not worth going to see.

— **Samuel Johnson**
(on visiting the Giants' Causeway in
Northern Ireland)

Washington is a city of Southern efficiency and Northern charm.

— **John F. Kennedy**

The darkest thing about Africa has always been our ignorance of it.

— **George Kimble**

If one had but a single glance to give the world, one should gaze on Istanbul.

— **Alphonse de Lamartine**

And suddenly there is Cagliari [the capital of Sardinia]: a naked town rising steep, steep, golden-looking piled naked to the sky from the plain at the head of the formless, hollow bay. It is strange and rather wonderful, not a bit like Italy.

— **D. H. Lawrence**

Canadians are Americans with no Disneyland.

— **Margaret Mahy**

People, houses, streets, animals, flowers — everything in Holland looks as if it were washed and ironed each night in order to glisten immaculately and newly started the next morning.

— **Felix Martí-Ibáñez**

Vienna is much like its women — it is beautiful, but it rarely smiles. Mozart wafts through the air with the smell of French perfume and cigarettes. Doormen wear top hats. Cyclists don't wear helmets. Shoes match bags. Bags match wallets. Even the dogs are designer. The only grubby thing in this impossibly beautiful city is me, and my boots — unfit for the cobblestone streets they traipse.

— **Marika McAdam**

It's all *real as far as I can see.*

— **Thomas Merton**
(on being asked if he had seen the "real Asia"
when visiting India)

*My most precious souvenir of Madagascar
is a small packet of red earth such as the
Malagasy take with them when they go
abroad ... to ensure their eventual return.*
— **Dervla Murphy**

The most beautiful place on earth.
— ***National Geographic Traveler***
(referring to the Dingle Peninsula, Ireland)

*If you ever go to New Mexico, it will itch
you for the rest of your life.*
— **Georgia O'Keefe**

*Those who have never been in the East
have missed the better part of the Earth.*
— **Robert Payne**

*I suggested that she take a trip
around the world.
"Oh, I know," returned the lady, yawning
with ennui, "but there's so many other
places I want to see first."*
— **S. J. Perelman**

*Here is the difference between Dante,
Milton and me. They wrote about
hell and never saw the place. I wrote
about Chicago after looking the town
over for years and years.*

— **Carl Sandburg**

*To drink in the spirit of a place you
should be not only alone but not
hurried.*

— **George Santayana**

Great God! This is an awful place.

— **Captain Robert Falcon Scott**
(at the South Pole)

*I think every wife has a right to insist
upon seeing Paris.*

— **Sydney Smith**

*Once a place becomes special,
it's no longer special.*

— **Peter Storey**

In Turkey it was always 1952, in Malaysia 1937; Afghanistan was 1910 and Bolivia 1949. It is twenty years ago in the Soviet Union, ten in Norway, five in France. It is always last year in Australia and next week in Japan.

— **Paul Theroux**
(in 1983)

It was great, best, best, best of all.... It was paradise. I just came back from paradise.

— **Dennis Tito**
(world's first "space tourist," on his return, 2001)

Angkor is not orchestral; it is monumental. It is an epic poem which makes its effect, like the Odyssey and like Paradise Lost, by the grandeur of its structure as well as by the beauty of the details ... and epic in rectangular forms imposed upon the Cambodian jungle.

— **Arnold Toynbee**

I find that, as a rule, when a thing is a wonder to us it is not because of what we see in it, but because of what others have seen in it. We get almost all our wonders at second hand ... By and by you sober down, and then you perceive that you have been drunk on the smell of somebody else's cork.

— **Mark Twain**

St. Peter's, Vesuvius, Heaven, Hell, everything that is much described is bound to be a disappointment at first experience.

— **Mark Twain**

Life is not measured by the number of breaths we take but by the places and moments that take our breath away.

— **Unknown**
(sometimes attributed in somewhat different form to George Carlin)

Monaco: Disneyland-sur-mer

— **Unknown**

*There are many famous monuments
in Europe that tourists should travel
hundreds of miles to miss.*

— **Unknown**

*Riding a horse through the flood
waters of Botswana's immense
Okavango Delta, close to elephants,
giraffes and the odd lion or two,
must rank as one of the world's most
exhilarating wildlife journeys.*

— **Steve Watkins and Clare Jones**

*Of course, America had often been
discovered before Columbus, but it
had always been hushed up.*

— **Oscar Wilde**

"You're home, dear. We don't have room service."

Coming Home, Looking Back

An American traveler abroad always comes home an ardent patriot.

— **American proverb**

*I've lived a life that's full,
I traveled each and every highway,
And more, much more than this,
I did it my way.*

— **Paul Anka**

Travel east or travel west, a man's own home is still the best.

— **Asian proverb**
(similar versions are found in other languages)

*The best part of the journey
is getting home.*
— **Canadian proverb**

*One always begins to forgive a place
as soon as it's left behind.*
— **Charles Dickens**

*Like all great travelers, I have seen
more than I remember, and remember
more than I have seen.*
— **Benjamin Disraeli**

He travels best that knows when to return.
— **English proverb**

*[For the English], holidays abroad are for
the looking forward to and the looking
back on, not for the actual enjoying.
Fun to prepare the plan of campaign for,
and to tell everyone about afterwards,
but hell to participate in.*
— **David Frost and Anthony Jay**

*Never any weary traveler complained that
he came too soon to his journey's end.*
— **Thomas Fuller**

*Ignorance about the world, consumerism/
materialism, fast pace of life, celebrity worship,
suburban sprawl, dependence on cars, higher
drinking age, ethnocentricity, work-centered
life and media pressure on women.*
— **Glimpse Study Abroad Acclimation Guide**
(citing the most difficult things for
U.S. students to adjust to on their return home
after studying abroad)

*Traveling: Either an experience we shall always
remember, or one we shall never forget.*
— **Julius Gordon**

*And who would be a traveler
And see the world afar,
What joys at Rome could equal home
Where my two children are?*
— **Edgar Guest**

There is a kind of latitude, they say, given to travelers to exceed the truth.
— **Eliza Haywood**

Here I am, safely returned over those peaks from a journey far more beautiful and strange than anything I had hoped for or imagined — how is it that this safe return brings such regret?
— **Peter Mattiessen**

Writing about travels is nearly always tedious, traveling being, like war and fornication, exciting but not interesting.
— **Malcolm Muggeridge**

I believe it was God's pleasure that we should get back in order that people might learn about the things that the world contains.
— **Marco Polo**

I have not told half of what I saw.
— **Marco Polo**

A traveler has a right to relate and embellish his experiences as he pleases, and it is very impolite to refuse that deference and applause they deserve.
— **Rudolf Erich Raspe**

Travel is the most private of pleasures. There is no greater bore than the travel bore. We do not in the least want to hear what he has seen in Hong Kong.
— **Vita Sackville-West**

A class of men who are exceedingly tiresome are those who, having traveled, talk of nothing but their adventures, the countries which they have seen or traversed, the dangers, whether real or fictitious, which they have encountered, repeat the same things an hundred times over.
— **St. John Baptist de la Salle**

Usually speaking, the worst-bred person in company is a young traveler just returned from abroad.
— **Jonathan Swift**

Travel is glamorous only in retrospect.
— **Paul Theroux**

*Only that traveling is good which reveals
to me the value of home, and enables me
to enjoy it better.*
— **Henry David Thoreau**

*So far as my experience goes, travelers
generally exaggerate the difficulties of the way.*
— **Henry David Thoreau**

He traveled in order to come home.
— **William Trevor**

*When I returned to the United States I
had horrible reverse culture shock. People
seemed so rude, the U.S. culture seemed
so fake compared to where I was living
previously, and Americans' love of fast food
disgusted me.*
— **Unidentified student who studied in the United
Arab Emirates**

The recounting of a journey and its ensuing mysteries and hardships is the oldest form of storytelling, and yet it never feels worn. In the telling, as well as in the going, there are good journeys and bad, yet the act of leaving the familiar to seek the unknown and the unpredictable ... remains timeless. We read about journeys of any age to find the world's edges and our own, to learn the best and worst of ourselves, to be scared witless, to bolster our courage, to be in awe.

— **Helen Whybrow**

I traveled among unknown men
In lands beyond the sea;
Nor, England! did I know till then
What love I bore to thee.

— **William Wordsworth**

PITFALLS & PROTECTIONS

The Weather Is Here, Wish You Were Beautiful

The Language Barrier

Americans who travel abroad for the first time are often shocked to discover that, despite all the progress that has been made in the last thirty years, many foreign people still speak in foreign languages.

— **Dave Barry**

England is a very popular foreign country to visit because the people there speak some English. Usually, however, when they get to the crucial part of a sentence they'll use words that they made up, such as "scone" and "ironmonger."

— **Dave Barry**

If somebody yells "Hey stranger!"
don't answer. Play deaf and dumb.
Even though you may know it,
don't speak the tongue.
— **Joseph Brodsky**

I'd love to speak fluent Italian. I'm actually
taking lessons. It's so frustrating. Three days
a week, a guy comes over to teach me. And
when he leaves, I don't know any Italian.
— **George Clooney**

Learn a new language and get a new soul.
— **Czech proverb**

No man should travel until he has learned
the language of the country he visits.
Otherwise, he voluntarily makes himself a
great baby — so helpless and so ridiculous.
— **Ralph Waldo Emerson**

A different language is a different
view of life.
— **Federico Fellini**

[T]he immediate reaction of an Englishman confronted with a European who does not understand him is to speak very slowly in baby talk and shout very loud, exactly the way they deal with the infantile and the senile.

— **David Frost and Anthony Jay**

Those who know nothing of foreign languages know nothing of their own.

— **Johann Wolfgang von Goethe**

I wish I weren't locked in my own language.

— **Carol Burdick Hudson**

The treachery of the phrase book ... is that you cannot begin to follow the answer to the question you've pronounced so beautifully — and worse still, your auditor now assumes you're fluent in Swahili.

— **Pico Iyer**

It was difficult for me to tell detailed stories or to just speak fluidly about random topics. I would get frustrated telling a story or be less likely to tell a story knowing I would most likely struggle. In hindsight I wish I would have taken more risks and been more carefree about speaking and less afraid to make mistakes.

— **Heather Keylon**
(who studied in Spain)

If you really have to speak to someone with little or no English … you can usually make yourself understood by speaking slowly but very loudly. Punctuate your words with little finger jabs into the foreigner's ribs to help him understand where the emphases fall.

— **Mark Leigh and Mike Lepine**

I speak Esperanto like a native.

— **Spike Milligan**

When you ask for fried eggs by making noises like a hen after laying, followed by noises like something sizzling in fat, the whole household [with whom you're staying] is convulsed with laughter, and not only are fried eggs served, but you are unanimously elected as one of the family.

— **Dervla Murphy**

Life is too short to learn German.

— **Richard Porson**

People thought that all Americans were loud and only speak one language. I learned the following joke: What do you call someone who speaks three or more languages? Multi-lingual. What do you call someone who speaks two languages? Bilingual. What do you call someone who speaks only one? American.

— **Alanna Randall**
(who studied in Costa Rica and France)

When describing our interests to our prospective host families, I said in Swahili, "Ninapenda-kuchesa," and did a little gyrating motion. I thought I had simply said, "I like to dance." My director pulled me aside soon afterward to let me know that the phrase is also slang for "I like to have sex." Needless to say, I was the last one picked for host families.

—Andrew Waggoner
(who studied in Tanzania)

Getting Lost & Other Hazards

*A traveler never gets lost
on a straight road.*
— **American proverb**

*When you arrive at
a fork in the road, take it.*
— **Yogi Berra**

*I can't say I was ever lost, but I was
bewildered once for three days.*
— **Daniel Boone**

*A ship in port is safe, but that is
not what ships are built for.*
— **Banazir Bhutto**

Half the fun of the travel is
the esthetic of lostness.

— **Ray Bradbury**

When traveling, there is no such thing as
bad experiences, only good stories.

— **Scott Cameron**

Your true traveler will not feel he has
had his money's worth unless he brings
back a few scars.

— **Lawrence Durrell**

Travel, and you get sick, sooner
or later. This truth is universal. I
remember reading somewhere that the
Queen of England, when she leaves
her country, always takes with her a
certain number of units of her own
blood.... Maybe that's just a myth.
The fact remains that if you travel,
no matter who you are, eventually
you will be brought low.

— **Ian Frazier**

You define your own horror journey, according to your taste. My definition of what makes a journey wholly or partially horrible is boredom.
— **Martha Gellhorn**

We will either find a way, or make one.
— **Hannibal**

Are you lost daddy I arsked [sic] tenderly. Shut up he explained.
— **Ring Lardner**

For forty years I have made a professional speciality of the happy journey. When things have gone wrong, I have resolutely forgotten them.
— **Jan Morris**

[T]hree times I have been shipwrecked, and for twenty-four hours I was adrift on the open sea. I have been constantly on the road; I have met dangers from rivers, dangers from robbers, dangers from my fellow-countrymen,

*dangers from foreigners, dangers in the town,
dangers in the wilderness, dangers at sea,
dangers from my fellow-Christians.*
— **Paul the Apostle**
(2 Corinthians 11:25-26, Revised English Bible)

*On the polar ice, we gladly hail the extreme cold,
as higher temperatures and light snow always
mean open water, danger and delay. Of course,
such minor incidents as frosted and bleeding
cheeks and noses we reckon as part of the great
game. Frosted heels and toes are far more serious,
because they lessen a man's ability to travel, and
traveling is what we are there for.*
— **Robert Peary**

*[T]ravel can be dangerous if you want it to be,
and it can be very safe if you want it to be. Even
in a war zone, which these days seems to be
everywhere except New Zealand or Greenland.*
— **Robert Young Pelton**

It's a bad plan that can't be changed.
— **Publilius Syrus**

*It is better to have traveled and gotten lost
than to never have traveled at all.*
— **George Santayana**

*Getting on the wrong train. Stopping
in an unknown town. Losing your
wallet, being arrested by mistake,
spending the night in prison.
Monsieur, it seems to me that you
could define adventure as an event
which is out of the ordinary without
being necessarily extraordinary.*
— **Jean-Paul Sartre**

*A problem is something you have hopes of
changing. Anything else is a fact of life.*
— **C. R. Smith**

*I could never test it [the warning that
Maine natives deliberately misdirect
travelers] because through my own efforts
I am lost most of the time without
any help from anyone.*
— **John Steinbeck**

*[T]he worst trips
make the best reading.*
— **Paul Theroux**

*No matter how far you have gone on
a wrong road, turn back.*
— **Turkish proverb**

*If you have some hard bumps, you are
probably traveling out of the rut.*
— **Unknown**

*There is no bad weather, only
inappropriate clothing.*
— **Unknown**
(variously attributed)

Travelers Aid

On packing: Lay out all your clothes and all your money. Then, take half the clothes and twice the money.
— **Susan Butler Anderson**

One all-purpose piece of advice regarding diplomacy and discretion in general conversation while overseas was given to us by a longtime American expatriate in the Far East: "Try to reply to questions as though your wealthy, elderly aunt had just asked you how much you think she should leave you in her will." In other words, always converse politely, with grace, tact and respect.
— **Roger E. Axtell**

Never trust anything you read in a travel article. Travel articles appear in publications that sell large, expensive advertisements to tourism-related industries, and these industries do not wish to see articles with headlines like: URUGUAY: DON'T BOTHER.

— **Dave Barry**

Never to travel any road a second time.

— **Ibn Battuta**
(a guiding principle of the 14th century
Arab traveler and geographer)

On my first trip abroad, years ago, a wise Englishman [said]: "In a foreign restaurant, never ask for a dish which you can get anywhere at home." What's the use of travel if you avoid new experiences?

— **John Erskine**

If [people who travel] tire themselves out on the very first day by rushing along, they will end up wasting many days as a result of sickness.

— **Evagius of Pontus**
(4th century A.D.)

If you will be a traveler, have always the eyes of a falcon, the ears of an ass, the face of an ape, the mouth of a hog, the shoulders of a camel, the legs of a stag, and see that you keep two bags very full, one of patience and another of money.

— **John Florio**
(in 1591; also attributed
in various forms to others)

I always travel to my destination with one carry-on bag (with wheels). There is more security knowing that I will have my clothes and documents with me. I am able to fit a three-week business wardrobe into the one carry-on.

— **Barbara R. Hauser**
(a Minneapolis attorney)

Try the famous echo in the British Museum reading room.

— **Gerard Hoffnung**
(offering deliberately bad advice
for visitors to Britain)

Most foreign tourists know that in London they are encouraged to take a piece of fruit, free of charge, from any open-air stall or display.

— **Michael Lipton**
(offering yet more deliberately bad advice for visitors to Britain)

Never eat Chinese food in Oklahoma.

— **Bryan Miller**

Beware of government sponsored stores and light operas. Limit yourself to one cathedral, one picture gallery and one giant Buddha a week.

— **Robert Morley**

Best way to combat traveler's diarrhea: If you can't peel it, cook it or boil it, forget it.

— **Peace Corps saying**
(attributed)

Most men in cultures around the world are honorable and respectful toward female travelers, but the few obnoxious exceptions

will always stand out. Sooner or later, you will get harassed, so be ready to deflect the harassment with a no-nonsense attitude — and never let it get to you emotionally.
— **Rolf Potts**

You can't pick a less crowded time to visit Disneyland than the period following Thanksgiving weekend and leading up to Christmas.
— **Bob Sehlinger**

Use this year's edition. People who try to save a few bucks by using an old book learn the seriousness of their mistake. Your trip costs you about $10 per waking hour. Your time is valuable. This guidebook saves lots of time.
— **Rick Steves**

Perhaps one of the only positive pieces of advice I was ever given was that supplied by an old courtier who observed: "Only two rules really count: never miss an opportunity to relieve yourself; never miss a chance to rest your feet."
— **The Duke of Windsor**

"According to the charts, it should be all clear sailing after this."

Travel Prayers

Protect me, O Lord;
My boat is so small,
And your sea is so big.
— **Breton prayer**

O God, who brought Abraham your son out of the land of the Chaldees, and preserved him unhurt through all his journeying, we beseech you to keep us your servants safe; be to us our support in setting out, our solace on the way, our shade in the heat, our shelter in the rain and cold, our transport in our weariness, our fortress in trouble, our staff in slippery paths, our harbor on stormy seas, that under your guidance we may safely reach our destination, and at length return home in safety.
— **The Book of Catholic Prayer**

That it may please Thee to preserve all who travel by land or by water.
— **The Book of Common Prayer**

He that will learn to pray, let him go to sea.
— **George Herbert**

God of the nomad and the pilgrim, may we find security in you and not in our possessions. May our homes be open to guests and our hearts to one another so that all our traveling is lighter and together we reach the goal.
— **Stephen Orchard**

A Tourist's Prayer:
O Lord, I don't want to be a spectator
A tour passenger looking out upon the real world
An audience to poverty and
want and homelessness.
Lord, involve me —
call me — implicate me — commit me
And Lord, help me to step off the bus.
— **Freda Rajotte**

We beseech Thee for those who are traveling from home, grant them an angel of peace as their fellow traveler, that they may receive no hurt from anyone, that they may finish their voyage and their travels in much cheerfulness.

—Sacramentary of Serapion
(4th century A.D.)

Alone with none but thee, my God,
I journey on my way.
What need I fear, when thou are near,
O King of night and day?
More safe am I within thy hand
Than if a host did round me stand.

—St. Columba
(translated by William T. Cairns)

OH, THE PEOPLE YOU'LL MEET!

"*I got my ticket for three dollars over the Internet.
Are you going to eat that salmon?*"

Tourists & Tourism

The precise origins of the word "tourist" are unclear. According to the French dictionary Le Petit Robert, the word was first coined in 1811 and introduced to France by Stendhal, who used it in 1838 in the title of his bestseller Les Mémoires d'un Touriste. *More recently, Jean-Didier Urbain, a specialist in the history of travel, revealed that the word was first used by an (unnamed) English writer in 1792.*

— **Rachael Antony and Joël Henry**

Try a volunteer vacation. The world will be a better place and so will you.

— **Ed Asner**

*I am leaving the town [St. Tropez] to the
invaders: increasingly numerous, mediocre,
dirty, badly behaved, shameless tourists.*
— **Brigitte Bardot**

*Modern tourist guides have helped
raise tourist expectations. And
they have provided the natives
— from Kaiser Wilhelm down to
the villagers of Chichicastenango —
with a detailed and itemized list of
what is expected of them and when.
These are the up-to-date scripts for
actors on the tourists' stage.*
— **Daniel Boorstin**

*The traveler used to go about the
world to encounter the natives.
A function of travel agencies now is
to prevent this encounter. They are
always devising efficient new ways
of insulating the tourist from the
travel world.*
— **Daniel Boorstin**

The cities of Italy [are] deluged with droves of these creatures, for they never separate, and you see them forty in number pouring along a street with their director — now in front, now at the rear, circling round them like a sheepdog.

— **British consular official in Italy**
(in 1865)

What an odd thing tourism is. You fly off to a strange land, eagerly abandoning all the comforts of home, and then expend vast quantities of time and money in a largely futile attempt to recapture the comforts that you wouldn't have lost if you hadn't left home in the first place.

— **Bill Bryson**

It is only Europeans who travel out of sheer curiosity.

— **Jean Chardin**

The traveler sees what he sees, the tourist sees what he has come to see.

— **G. K. Chesterton**

The cuckoo clock, in fact, may be said to be the quintessential souvenir, in that it exists purely to be bought, sold, wrapped, carried home, unwrapped and put in lofts.

— **Alan Coren**

Tourism is the march of stupidity. You're expected to be stupid. The entire mechanism of the host country is geared to travelers acting stupidly. You walk around dazed, squinting into fold-out maps. You don't know how to talk to people, how to get anywhere, what the money means, what time it is, what to eat or how to eat it…. You are an army of fools, wearing bright polyesters, riding camels, taking pictures of each other, haggard, dysenteric, thirsty. There is nothing to think about but the next shapeless event.

— **Don DeLillo**

Traveling as a volunteer departs from conventional adventure travel and cultural immersion experiences by serving, and thereby learning first hand about the host community, often in an unconventional setting. It is a true exchange of ideas, cultures and hopes for the future.

— **Elderhostel**

The average tourist wants to go to places where there are no tourists.

— **Sam Ewing**

As a member of an escorted tour you don't even have to know the Matterhorn isn't a tuba.

— **Temple Fielding**

Who was it who said, "He is a tourist, you are a holidaymaker, but I am a traveler"?

— **Steven Fry and Hugh Laurie**

An explorer seeks the undiscovered; a traveler seeks that which has been discovered by the mind working in history; and the tourist seeks that which has been discovered by entrepreneurship and prepared for him by the arts of mass publicity.

— **Paul Fussell**

Tourism soothes you by comfort and familiarity and shields you from the shocks of novelty and oddity. It confirms your prior view of the world instead of shaking it up. Tourism requires that you see conventional things, and that you see them in a conventional way.

— **Paul Fussell**

The country of the tourist pamphlet always is another country, an embarrassing abstraction of the desirable that, thank God, does not exist on this planet, where there are always ants and bad smells and empty Coca Cola bottles to keep the grubby finger-print of reality upon the beautiful.

— **Nadine Gordimer**

Mass tourists ask little except the same sort of food that they eat at home; the English, for example, scorn any meal that does not include potatoes — to hell with rice and spaghetti! And who wants wine, when he can get beer? They don't object to a little local color, especially flamenco-strumming by pretended gypsies, and gaudy souvenirs; … olive-wood bowls and boxes, bullfighting posters with their own names printed between those of El Litri and James Ostos … But they shy away from any closer approach to the real Spain.

— **Robert Graves**

The obvious customers for medical tourism are the uninsured, who have to pay the entire cost of their care … Economists used to say that health care was the one thing that couldn't be outsourced. Shortly after, American medical centers started sending X-rays to India for analysis. It was just a matter of time before the patients followed their photos.

— **Froma Harrop**

Travelers are those who leave their assumptions at home and [tourists are] those who don't.

— **Pico Iyer**

Of all noxious animals ... the most noxious is a tourist. And of all tourists, the most vulgar, ill-bred, offensive and loathsome is the British tourist.
— **Francis Kilvert**
(April 1870 diary entry)

A tourist is an ugly human being.
— **Jamaica Kincaid**

"Never change a winner" is an old rule in the tourist industry, and there is an amazing continuity in the structure of package tours to the Mediterranean, among localities and tour companies alike. The format gives veteran tourists a comforting or irritating feeling of déjà vu: they know exactly what to expect of their week. Again, it is the pioneer experiences from Majorca and the Costa del Sol that set the standards. Transnationalized, the Spanish experience frames the Greek or Tunisian charter week, from the idea of the welcoming drink to the final village fiesta.
— **Orvar Löfgren**

In 1851 Mr. Thomas Cook invented the holiday tour industry by discovering that he could get reduced rates from the railway if he took his teetotal party from Leicester to Loughborough in one lump. From this he progressed to taking parties of teetotalers on guided tours of the Continent. The next step was taking non-teetotalers on guided tours of the Continent.

— **Frank Muir**

Most travelers content themselves with what they may chance to see from car-windows, hotel verandahs, or the deck of a steamer ... clinging to the battered highways like drowning sailors to a life raft.

— **John Muir**

The weather is here; wish you were beautiful.

— **Postcard greeting, source unknown**

What I hadn't realized was how very closely the world of the resort hotel resembles that of the preschool. The young women who run the concierge desk are the controlling grown-ups; they set the curriculum and sort out the squabbles. The indignant fifty-five-year-old guest, in his beach romperwear, with bulging face and shrilling voice, is pure 200-pound toddler in a snit.

— **Jonathan Raban**

The vagabond, when rich, is called a tourist.

— **Paul Richard**

Political serenity, not scenic or cultural attractions, constitute[s] the first and central requirement of tourism.

— **L. K. Richter and W. L. Waugh**

We [American tourists], unfortunately, don't make a good impression collectively ... There ought to be a law prohibiting over three Americans going anywhere abroad together.

— **Will Rogers**

Winter is coming and tourists will soon be looking for a place to mate.
— **Will Rogers**

I sometimes think that Thomas Cook should be numbered among the secular saints. He took travel from the privileged and gave it to the people.
— **Robert Runcie**
(former Archbishop of Canterbury)

In the Middle Ages, people were tourists because of their religion, whereas now they are tourists because tourism is their religion.
— **Robert Runcie**

The tourism "product" is not the tourist destination, but it is about experiences of that place and what happens there.
— **Chris Ryan**

As the sherpa said to Edmund Hillary on the slopes of Mount Everest, some people travel only to look, while others come to see.
— **Patricia Schultz**

[Englishmen] have a reputation for pugnacity in France; let them therefore be especially cautious not to make use of their fists, however grave the provocation, otherwise they will rue it. No French magistrate or judge will listen to any plea of provocation; fine and imprisonment are the offender's inevitable portion.

— **Mariana Starke**
(in *A Guide for Travellers on the Continent*,
the first modern travel guide,1820)

In a café in [the island of] Rhodes three Englishwomen walked in wearing the most outlandish holiday clothes and Panama hats, with lots of raincoats and cameras and walking sticks and rucksacks. They stood about looking for a waiter and one said in a loud voice, "How do we attract attention?"

— **Elizabeth Taylor**
(the British novelist)

Tourists don't know where they've been, travelers don't know where they're going.

— **Paul Theroux**

Tourists capture the image of a well-known place in a photo but miss its essence; the anti-tourist dismisses the place as a cliché and misses the whole thing; while the traveler grasps its majesty.
— **John Thorn**

Tourism depends on economic development and open, free societies.
— **Graham Todd**

Why is it that a tourist will travel thousands of miles to get away from people, only to send postcards saying "Wish you were here"?
— **Unknown**

Swedes abroad do not want to be abroad. They would rather be at home. This is seen in the way they often travel in groups, book into dreadful, fenced Swedish tour company ghettoes (with Swedish radio stations), and immediately seek out other Swedes, hunt for Swedish food, Swedish coffee, Swedish newspapers, anything at all so long as it is Swedish. "Why do they travel?" one may wonder. The main reason is that Sweden is rarely sunny and Swedes love the sun. There we have the basic problem. Swedes do not really go to Spain, Greece or Florida. They go to the sun....

— ***Veckojournalen***
(Swedish magazine, 1994)

Guests at the Hilton Hotel are frequently reduced to dialing room service to find out which country they are in.

— **John Wells**

The Caribbean holiday, after all, is a mass-marketed product as well as a place ... The "destination," as they say in the business, is an integral part of the identity of the Caribbean holiday product at the same time as it's strangely irrelevant: basically anything with sun and palm trees will do.

— **Alexander Wilson**

Traveling Companions

Tell me with whom you travel and I'll tell you who you are.
— **American proverb**

It is easier to find a traveling companion than to get rid of one.
— **Art Buchwald**

If hell is other people, purgatory, some would say, is perpetual train travel in the company of other people.
— **Rosemary Burton**

A journey is best measured in friends rather than miles.
— **Tim Cahill**

I've been married and divorced six times ... My wives all said they loved travel, but they were thinking the QEII and the Ritz, not riding some dirty boat from one godforsaken island to another.

— **John D. Clouse**
(who in 1995 held the Guinness Book of Records
for the most traveled person)

But why, oh why, do the wrong people travel, When the right people stay at home.

— **Noël Coward**

That man travels to no purpose who sits down alone to his meals.

— **John Davis**

Travel only with thy equals or thy betters; if there are none, travel alone.

— **The Dhammapada**

One of the pleasantest things in the world is going on a journey; but I like to go by myself.

— **William Hazlitt**

Never go on trips with anyone you do not love.

— **Ernest Hemingway**

Traveling in the company of those we love is home in motion.

— **Leigh Hunt**

One travels more usefully when alone because he reflects more.

— **Thomas Jefferson**

He travels fastest who travels alone.

— **Rudyard Kipling**

The only use of a gentleman in traveling is to look after the luggage.

— **Emily Lowe**
(in 1857)

Gender often forms a bond between women travelers. Women confide in each other.

— **Mary Morris**

The tight compartment fills; our careful eyes
Go to explore each other's destinies.
— **Harold Munro**

Traveling with anyone is a very ticklish
business … What is your thrill may be my
bore … I cannot imagine what fire and
pillage I would commit if anyone were in a
position to keep me looking at things longer
than I wanted to look.
— **Cornelia Stratton Parker**

Infants are easy travelers. As long as they
are fed and comfortable, there is really no
limit to what you can do when on the road
with little ones. Food plus adequate rest is
the perfect formula for happy babies.
— **Bob Sehlinger**

I was born and raised in a neighborhood
called Noah's Ark. If you didn't travel in
pairs, you just didn't travel.
— **Stanley Shapiro**

The man who goes alone can start today;
but he who travels with another must wait
till that other is ready.

— **Henry David Thoreau**

I have found out that there ain't no surer
way of finding out whether you like people
or hate them, than to travel with them.

— **Mark Twain**

Bring a novel on the plane to protect
yourself against chatty strangers.

— **Anne Tyler**

Good company in a journey
makes the way to seem shorter.

— **Izaak Walton**

I Mary-Lou, take thee Larry, to by my
constant traveling companion, to Hong and
to Kong, in Cyclades and in Delft, for deck
class or deluxe, so long as we both can move.

— **Mary-Lou Weisman**

Some marriages are saved by going on vacation. While the marriage is at home, the partners may be contemplating divorce, but send that marriage on vacation and they're on a second honeymoon. On the other hand, a marriage that gets along swimmingly at home can be a fish out of water on vacation.

— **Mary-Lou Weisman**

Questions Tourists Ask

- How far above sea level are we? (asked by a cruise passenger)
- What time is the midnight buffet?
- Is that the same moon we see at home?
- Why did the Greeks build so many ruins?
- How many miles of undiscovered cave are there?
- How much does it cost to mail a letter to the U.S.? (from an American tourist in Hawaii)
- Why is the "Closed for cleaning" sign on the rest room?
- When do they turn off the waterfalls? (at Yosemite National Park)
- Are the coconuts in the trees real?
- How come all of the war battles were fought in National Parks?
- Windsor Castle is beautiful, but why did they build it so close to the airport?
- If it rains, will the fireworks be held inside?

"What fire? We're fleeing eco-tourists."

Ecotourists

Because we depend on so many detailed and subtle aspects of the environment, any change imposed on it for the sake of some economic benefit has a price ... Sooner or later, wittingly or unwittingly, we must pay for every intrusion on the natural environment.

— **Barry Commoner**

How much more tourism can the island [of Bali] take? How much more traffic? How many more craft shops? ... How many more jets? The answer is it never stops, the roads are widened, the hotels multiply, the direct flights increase ... It is now clear that the unbelievably complex social and religious

*fabric of the Balinese is at last breaking
down under the tourist onslaught. Inflation,
freeloading, and other social ills have sprung up,
and along with relative affluence have come the
breakdown of traditional values.*
— **B. Dalton**

*Ecotourism means you take your ethics with
you when you travel. It is environmentally
and politically correct.*
— **EcoSource**

*Even tourism, once considered the ideal
"clean" industry, has run afoul of the no-
trespassing mood in places.*
— ***Forbes** magazine*

*[T]ourism, through crowding, wear,
litter, economic and psychological impacts,
can cause as much contamination and
degradation of the general atmosphere and
environment as any physical process that is
not actually physically harmful.*
— **Herman Kahn and Anthony J. Wiener**

A thing is right when it tends to preserve the integrity, stability and beauty of the biotic community. It is wrong when it tends otherwise.

— **Aldo Leopold**

[The National Park Service] shall ... conserve the scenery and the natural and historic objects and the wildlife therein and to provide for the enjoyment of the same in such manner and by such means as will leave them unimpaired for the enjoyment of future generations.

— **National Park Service Organic Act**
(1916)

We do not inherit the land from our ancestors; we borrow it from our children.

— **Native American proverb**

In seeking the unspoiled, you inevitably spoil it.

— **George Packer**

*We have to define the maximum load,
the point beyond which damages
will become irreparable.*
— **Gernot Patzelt**
(commenting on Alpine tourism in 1984)

*All too often "responsible travel" is a
notion that gets hijacked by ecotourism
marketers and political demagogues.
Fortunately, responsible travel doesn't
require that you become an ecotour
client or a shrill activist…. [F]or all
the talk about ecological and cultural
sustainability, few people actually
understand these concepts. Knowing your
science — not your politics — is what
will best inform your decisions as you
tread lightly through the world.*
— **Rolf Potts**

*Our society will be defined not only
by what we create, but what we
refuse to destroy.*
— **John C. Sawhill**

Take nothing but pictures. Leave nothing but footprints. Kill nothing but time.
— **Unknown**

[E]cotourism is the only tourism development that is sustainable in the long run.
— **J. A. N. Warren and C. N. Taylor**

[Ecotourists are] expecting discovery and enlightenment from the ecotourism experience. Personal growth in emotional, spiritual as well as intellectual terms appear to be expected outcomes from ecotourism travel for the majority of these travelers.
— **P. Williams**

"Carrying capacity" — The level of visitor use an area can accommodate with high levels of satisfaction for visitors and few impacts on resources.
— **World Tourism Organization**

"Sustainable tourism" — [Development which] meets the needs of present tourists and host regions while protecting and enhancing opportunities for the future. It is envisaged as leading to management of all resources in such a way that economic, social and aesthetic needs can be fulfilled while maintaining cultural integrity, essential ecological processes, biological diversity, and life support systems.

— **World Tourism Organization**

Students Abroad

I integrated into a community. I didn't just visit Chile. When I left, part of me was left there, and part of Chile came with me.

— Alexandra Auld
(who studied in that country)

[T]oo few American students study abroad, in part because too few study second languages; fewer yet study them to the point of mastery; equally, and, more to the point, those who do study abroad study too little, too late. Why? The short answer is "culture;" American culture does not reward — nor does it provide incentives for — study abroad.

— Denis Doyle
(in 2000)

The 18th century gentleman culminated his education with the "grand tour," a year-long ramble through Europe. My own year in Vienna, however, served not as the climax of my education, but the beginning.

— **Clark Hendley**

Four rules for students traveling on off-campus programs:
- *No whining*
- *Don't be late*
- *Find and use a restroom before things reach crisis proportions, and*
- *Look out for each other.*

— **Gordon S. Jackson**

Best parts of my experience: Hiking and backpacking in the Amazon rainforest, an orchestra trip to Brasil, traveling to Suriname over Christmas Break, and seeing giant leatherback turtles lay their eggs on the beach.

— **Lindsey Kiehn**
(who studied in French Guiana)

Mom and Dad:
Thanks for giving me the world.

— **Unknown**

(sign held up at the Great Wall of China by student on a
Semester at Sea round-the-world program)

My heart has grown and my mind has
expanded. I am forever changed.

— **Blythe Wyatt**

(after her Semester at Sea voyage in spring 2005)

I Should've Stayed Home!

"The guide book says it's the best B.& B. in the Carpathians."

*I have recently been all round the world
and have formed a very poor opinion of it.*
— **Thomas Beecham**

Never go abroad. It's a dreadful place.
— **Earl of Cardigan**

*Why do people so love to wander?
I think the civilized parts of the world will
suffice for me in the future.*
— **Mary Cassatt**

*I am weary of traveling and am resolved to
go abroad no more.*
— **King Charles II of England**
(attributed)

*It is not fit that every man should travel; it
makes a wise man better and a fool worse.*
— **Owen Feltham**

*If an ass goes traveling
he will not come home a horse.*
— **Thomas Fuller**

I wouldn't mind seeing China if I could come back the same day. I hate being abroad.

— **Philip Larkin**

What people travel for is a mystery.

— **T. B. Macaulay**

I don't mind going someplace just so long as I can be home for lunch.

— **Charles Schulz**

[W]hen I was at home, I was in a better place; but travelers must be content.

— **William Shakespeare**

It is not worthwhile to go around the world to count the cats in Zanzibar.

— **Henry David Thoreau**

Travel? Why should I? I live here.

— **Unknown Bostonian**

THE END

Index

N

O

P

R

Resources

Below are the main anthologies of quotations on which this volume relies. The travel books consulted were too numerous to list.

American Heritage Dictionary of American Quotations

American Quotations, Gorton Carruth and Eugene Ehrlich

Camp's Unfamiliar Quotations, Wesley D. Camp

The Cassell Dictionary of Contemporary Quotations

Cassell's Book of Humorous Quotations

Chambers Dictionary of Quotations

Chicken Soup for the Traveler's Soul, Jack Canfield et. al.

Collins Quotation Finder

The Concise Columbia Dictionary of Quotations, Robert Andrews

The Crown Treasury of Relevant Quotations

Dictionary of American Proverbs, Wolfgang Mieder

Dictionary of Foreign Quotations, Robert Collison

A Dictionary of Quotations, A. Norman Jeffares and Martin Gray

Dictionary of Quotations, Bergen Evans

The Dictionary of Quotations, Ted Smart

En Carta Dictionary of Quotations

Familiar Quotations, John Bartlett

The Fitzhenry and Whiteside Book of Quotations, Robert I. Fitzhenry

Flinging Monkeys at the Coconuts, Trevor Craille

Friendly Advice, Jon Winokur

The Guinness Dictionary of Yet More Poisonous Quotations, Colin Jarman

Home Book of Proverbs, Maxims and Familiar Phrases

The International Thesaurus of Quotations, Rhoda Tripp

The Left-Handed Dictionary, Leonard Levinson

The Multicultural Dictionary of Proverbs, Harold V. Cordry

Never Scratch a Tiger with a Short Stick: And Other Quotes for Leaders, Gordon S. Jackson

A New Dictionary of Quotations, H. L. Mencken

The New Dictionary of Thoughts

The New Penguin Dictionary of Modern Quotations

The New York Public Library Book of Twentieth Century American Quotations

The Official Rules and Explanations, Paul Dickson

Outside Insights, Gordon Jackson

The Oxford Book of Aphorisms, John Gross

The Oxford Dictionary of Phrase, Saying, and Quotations

The Oxford Dictionary of Quotations

The Oxford Dictionary of Humorous Quotations

The Oxford Dictionary of Modern Quotations

The Oxford Dictionary of Political Quotations

The Pan Dictionary of Famous Quotations

The Penguin Dictionary of Quotations

The Penguin Dictionary of Modern Quotations

The Penguin Dictionary of Modern Humorous Quotations

The Quotable Quotations Book, Alec Lewis

The Quotable Woman

Quotations for Our Time, also published as *Peter's Quotations*, Laurence Peter

Simpson's Contemporary Quotations, James B. Simpson

The Toastmaster's Treasure Chest, Herbert V. Prochnow and Herbert V. Prochnow Jr.

The Viking Book of Aphorisms, W. H. Auden and Louis Kronenberger

What the Dormouse Said, Amy Gish

The Wordsworth Dictionary of Quotations

Who Said What

The Whole World Book of Quotations

Words of Wisdom, William Safire and Leonard Safir

21ˢᵗ Century Dictionary of Quotations

20,000 Quips and Quotes, Evan Esar